The Driving Force Within: A Roadmap to Business

Terry Back

This book is dedicated to all business owners, especially those who own salons and spas, who strive so hard to grow their businesses and change lives.

Main Entrance to High Tech Salon & Spa

Logo for My Current Salon & Spa, High Tech

A Row of Styling Stations in High Tech

Index

Introduction...5

Chapter 1: Leadership.................................7

Chapter 2: Having a Plan.........................14

Chapter 3: Location.................................20

Chapter 4: Preparing to Own Your Business:

Building or Buying Your Building..............28

Chapter 5: Build-Out Cost.......................41

Chapter 6: Equipment Costs &

Improvements...48

Chapter 7: Choosing Your Products.......59

Chapter 8: Choosing Employees.............67

Chapter 9: Marketing..............................77

Chapter 10: Financial Planning..............89

Chapter 11: Daily Operations.................95

Chapter 12: Building Success for Guest

Coordinators...105

Chapter 13: Challenges & Statistics to Keep in

Mind..112

Chapter 14: Growing Your Profit Margin...........118

Planning for Book #2.............................124

Acknowledgments.................................125

References...127

Introduction

As an eight-year-old boy, I sold lollipops and fireballs from my locker and did not yet realize that I was an entrepreneur who would have an impact on the business world. My father always told me, "Whatever you want in life there is always a door open. If not, there is a little crack, so find a way to get through it." In the business world this means to never give up when you are on your venture.

There are opportunities that face us every day. I love the saying by Sir Richard Branson, the self-made billionaire who owns Virgin Group, "If you don't have the right experience to reach your goal, look for another way in. Keep your eyes open. Look and learn. You don't have to go to art school to be a fashion designer. Join a fashion company and push a broom. Work your way up." What this tells you, as an entrepreneur, is that you can start at the bottom and work your way to ultimate success.

While you read my book, I hope that it will drive you to grow your opportunities daily and give you an understanding that, as entrepreneurs, our daily walk can change our lives, and we can help so many people succeed in life. As coaches, we can make a difference in the lives of others, and it is our mission to do so. I am so grateful knowing that life is like the beautiful blue sky and that the sun is so full of warmth; God is good.

The Beginning

Imagine the first day of elementary school. Your mother walks you into the school building. You fear the unknown but also feel excitement. You meet your teacher for the first time. This experience and the many more you have at school will impact you for days, months, and years. Knowing this — how greatly an experience, even a seemingly small one, can change your life — can make the first day of school the most exciting day of your life; you dream about what school will be like as you step into the unknown.

The feelings you have on your first day of school are similar to the feelings you will have or that you have had the day you decide or decided to open your first business. These are the feelings of stepping outside of your box or comfort zone. In the words of Sir Richard Branson, "One thing is certain in business. You and everyone around you will make mistakes." Mistakes are a part of life, and we are humans.

When you start your business venture, never give up, and remember that this venture is your dream. There are a lot of what I call "dream-stealers" out there in the world. Therefore, remember your business dreams and that entrepreneurs never just walk away; they have a plan and are great leaders.

Chapter 1: Leadership

The mark of a good leader is loyal followers. Leadership is nothing without a following. – Proverbs 14:28

Take charge. As an entrepreneur, you are taking a direction in life in which you will impact many people's lives.

Knowing that you were born to be a leader and showing strong leadership skills are important. At the age of of eighteen, when I became a hairdresser, I knew that I could change the world and change people's lives forever. This is how you need to feel when you have great passion for success. When I started my first company at twenty-one years old, I was driven by my passion for success.

My drive also came from my family. My father used to tell me that I was born to be a leader. My parents adopted four children, including me, from all different families, and this pushed me to do well.

When I opened my first company, I had the pleasure of meeting a man who was a business consultant. During the time of his service, he asked me, "Who handles your profit and loss statements and your income and expense reports?" I replied, "What is that?" I hired him to teach me, and he was my business consultant for ten years.

Even though I felt that I was a very talented hairdresser, I knew nothing about business. This is what happens to so many business owners; we become caught up in the egotism of ownership, but we forget the large picture, which requires us to know something about business. Because I wanted to learn more about business, I surrounded myself with amazing mentors. These mentors took me into a business direction that changed my life forever.

> *Remember: nothing ventured, nothing gained*

Always remember that, as entrepreneurs, we are the self-driven people who can make the biggest differences in many people's lives. When we are put into leadership positions, we strive to succeed in many ways.

When you begin in the world of success, give it your all and never give up. When I first started in a salon, I had zero clientele, and no one knew me. I had to grow from nothing, so I volunteered my time to different events. I volunteered for any events that I could, such as ladies groups. Each time these different groups would see or hear my name they would remember my talent.

I see so many young, talented stylists and artists who are in training to become certified and want to open their own businesses. However, as an entrepreneur, before you lead your own business you need to have a stable clientele and great cash flow, which will help you be a more stable owner. The employees who you hire need to know that you invest time and commitment in your company, and it is your job as a leader to coach others to gain success. When you – as an owner – are involved with growing your team, you gain more credibility in your team's eyes. Even if something goes wrong, you want this credibility with your team to remain. Try to make plans for potential problems ahead of time. When something does go wrong, do not show fear in front of your team because it is a sign of weakness in leadership.

Additionally, in the world of business, you should never let your ego get in the way of success. As a leader, you are in a position that is vital for your company and employees. When I started my company, I had this unexplainable rush. However, I came back to reality very quickly when I realized that I had to make major decisions that could impact everyone in my company.

> *I always take business very seriously, and you should too.*

You are reading this book for a reason: you want to improve your leadership skills, so take control. Review every employee's performance and consistently look at their customer retention rates. I discuss this more in depth in *Chapter 11: Daily Operations*. The rest of this book will provide you with more of a breakdown on every aspect of your business.

Notes

13

Chapter 2: Having a Plan

I live by the saying, "If you fail to plan, you plan to fail."

Your roadmap is your plan; your roadmap is where you are going in life. Always have a strategy that can change your roadmap. You need to devote time to researching and planning because, even though you are an entrepreneur who can make a difference in the business world, you might not know where to begin.

You need direction and guidance, but you also need to remember that the world of business is very challenging. You need to structure a roadmap or business plan for your company. For example, let's say that you are searching for a franchise but don't know how to begin. Websites, such as FranchiseOpportunities.com, can help you decide which direction to take.

For help finding a business plan that fits your needs visit businessplanupdate.com.

If you decide to open a company, make sure you know enough ahead of time about the particular type of business that you want to start, make a business plan, and implement your plan. Your business plan tells your story. You need to show lenders or investors that you have prepared a plan for your business and that you will have a way to pay lenders back. Lenders want to see your strategy for making your business successful. A business plan is like Phase 1 of a roadmap: it gives you the direction to start your plan. Phase 2 is starting your financial direction.

As I mentioned in Chapter 1, if your plan is to go in the direction of being a business owner, you need to have money to begin, so let me explain what I mean. When you know how much money you have to put toward your business, it is easier to create your budget regardless of whether you are opening your first, second, or third business. I hear about so many young entrepreneurs who want to venture out and open their own companies, but they do not have business plans in place. Even if they have capital from a loved one or a cosigner for a loan, they have serious issues if they do not have experience, clientele, or cash flow, and, without these three requirements, they will exhaust all of their resources. Therefore, before you start your business, make sure you have a strong clientele and five to seven years of experience in a salon and spa. This gives you a strong cushion in business and will help you take your business in the right direction.

Owners know that creating a strategy is the golden rule. If you don't know where to begin just ask. That's right: ask. Link yourself with very successful business owners in your profession and in other business areas. This is what I did not only with salon and spa owners but with realtors and investors in the stock market. Be diverse in your business planning because, as you will keep hearing me say, we, as entrepreneurs, succeed in many areas.

Never be afraid to succeed, my friends. My contact information is included at the end of this book, so reach out to me if you have any questions relating to business or real-estate. I will do my best to help you and lead you in the right direction.

Notes

Chapter 3: Location

Location, location, location!

Look at geographical studies and statistics, such as local demographics, to help you decide on your business location. Do you need a heavily trafficked area for exposure, or do you need to be away from the main street to make your business successful? Remember that all properties subject to cities and locations are negotiable when it comes to cost per square foot. A building in a high traffic area has higher costs than a building located farther away from a main road. Therefore, it is important to plan properly when it comes to location.

When deciding on a location, go to your town or city government agencies and find out if there are any changes being made around the area you are considering for your new business. For example, let's say that a town or city's road patterns are going to be changed. This can impact the traffic that you are depending on for your business. If you have already signed a long lease, but a traffic pattern changes, this can devastate your company. However, if you have

20

spent a few years building your reputation, you can save a lot of money because you can succeed even if your business is away from a main street where the cost per square foot of a building is not as high. Additionally, buildings away from the main street may be more negotiable in terms of price.

If your location is on the main street, your costs will be higher. When I started my first business, it was in a strip center, which was very visible from the road. However, in 1986, it was much easier to build a very strong business than it is today. As years and businesses progress, we as entrepreneurs are challenged in many ways, and business locations can make or break us. This is why, when I started, I did my research. I went to my chamber of commerce, local government, and city business inspectors to find out any information that I needed for my business venture. You need to do your research on the area where you want your business too.

> *Remember: entrepreneurs have the internal drives to always chase after their dreams, but be careful. Even though you may be very savvy in the business world, there are some people I call "the devil's roadblocks" who will try to put a stop to your dreams.*

Let's say that you are considering buying a building in a historical district. Historical districts are sometimes part of enterprise zones. An enterprise zone is a section of businesses in a particular location which may allow business owners in the area to have specific tax breaks and exceptions from certain government regulations. Before deciding on a location, you need to research ahead of time because you can earn tax benefits if your business will be in an enterprise zone, and these benefits can help you with purchasing and renovating the property. When I purchased a building in a historical district, I was so excited because I did not have to buy business licenses for five years, which was a major benefit. When you consider buying a building, check with your local government office and review their benefits.

Within the first fifteen years of my business, I moved my location three times because I wanted to take my company to the next level by expanding. My third move was when I purchased a historical property in an enterprise zone. I owned the property for ten years, and within the property I had two beautiful loft apartments, offices that I leased out on the third floor, and my salon was on the first and second floors. The building was a perfect fit for the business until there were major issues with parking. The city had a very large parking lot connected to our building, but, after we would validate parking tickets for our clients, five years would end up costing us $25,000. I was even more driven after I started losing clients due to limited parking, and it was beneficial for me to buy another piece of property to build another building.

Historical Property in Staunton, Virginia

When you are considering your location, always plan for the future for your business. When reviewing potential business locations, talk to your prospective neighbors and try to find answers to any questions you have about road and walkway traffic. My goal is to always provide you with multiple ways to see your businesses grow.

<u>Notes</u>

Chapter 4: Preparing to Own Your Business: Building or Buying Your Building

You want your company to grow, and by building or buying a building for your business, there is potential for tremendous growth. This growth is not only in your business but in your venture into the world of real-estate. To achieve this growth, read my business plan very carefully.

In terms of legal information and advice, it is very important that you consult with an attorney to receive the best information that you can for your situation and the type of business you want to grow. It is also very important for your business to have a good certified public accountant (CPA). After you have been approved by lenders, you will need an attorney to prepare your corporation.

To begin, set up an appointment with a corporate attorney. He or she can set up a Limited Liability Corporation/Company (LLC). An LLC "is a type of business entity that combines the personal liability protection of a corporation with the tax benefits and simplicity of a partnership" (legalzoom.com). More specifically, an LLC is a "non-corporate business whose owners actively participate in the organization's management and are protected against personal liability for the organization's debts and obligations." An LLC "is a hybrid legal entity that has both the characteristics of a corporation and of a partnership," and it "provides its owners with corporate-like protection against personal liability" (dictionary.law.com). An LLC gives you growth in your net worth with your company and in real-estate.

For example, you might set up an LLC and buy a building with the potential of adding tenants. Additional tenants can help create positive cash flow, which means less debt and more growth for your business. Because of this opportunity for growth and others, it is important to try to think outside of the box about what you can do with a commercial building before your buy or build it.

As I mention in *Chapter 3: Location*, I bought my first building and was able to make significant profit with it because I used the building in multiple ways, which caused more growth for my business. Additionally, the gentleman who initially showed the building to me offered me owner financing. Owner financing is when you sign a contract with an owner and pay the owner instead of signing a contract with a bank and paying money to the bank; this can be very beneficial to both parties. Owner financing was beneficial in my case because I had to put very little money down and was offered a three-year balloon on the sale agreement. After three years, I had to get financing from a lending company. However, by this time, I had a positive track record for the payments I had made, and I had cash flow from my property. Because of these factors, it was very easy for me to transfer the remaining loan to the bank. At this time, I was only twenty-eight years old, and I had very little collateral.

There is so much to know about corporations that it is best to speak to a corporate attorney or tax accountant to effectively and correctly know which directions to take.

Once an attorney prepares your corporation, it will be an S corporation.

An S corporation is a corporation that elects to be treated as a pass-through entity (like a sole proprietorship or partnership) for tax purposes. Since all corporate income is "passed through" directly to the shareholders who include the income on their individual tax returns, S corporations are not subject to double taxation. Moreover, the accounting for an S corporation is generally easier than for a C corporation (legalzoom.com).

The basic difference between an S corporation and a C corporation is that a C corporation's profits are taxed at two levels. This taxation is commonly referred to as "double taxation." The first tax is that a C corporation pays a corporate tax on its corporate income. The second tax is that a C corporation distributes profits to shareholders who pay income tax on those dividends. This is why creating an S corporation, instead of a C corporation, can be beneficial; it can help you avoid the double taxation of a C corporation if you elect with the IRS to be taxed as an S corporation. Your attorney can help you figure out what type of corporation is needed for your specific business.

Setting up a corporation helps with taxes and liabilities for your company. To illustrate, let's use an example of a company that earns $100,000. With a sole proprietorship, a business owner who is married and filing jointly with his or her spouse would be in the 25% income tax bracket. With this corporation, assume the business owners take $50,000 in salary and leave $50,000 in the corporation as a corporate profit. The federal corporate tax is 15% on the first $50,000. Now, the business owner is in the 15% tax bracket for his or her personal income tax. This can reduce a business owner's tax liability by over $8,000.

Additionally, there are fringe benefits to setting up a corporation. A corporation can provide corporate retirement and medical plans as well as greater retirement and life insurance contribution limits than unincorporated entities. Consult with your accountant or tax advisor when establishing an employee benefit package for your corporation.

In a corporation, there are no limits of restrictions on the amount of capital or the operating losses that a corporation may carry back to subsequent tax years. Unincorporated entities, however, are subject to more stringent rules regarding corporate losses. For example, a sole proprietor cannot claim a capital loss greater than $3,000 unless he or she has offsetting capital gains.

Another tool many people use to reduce their overall tax liability is leasing assets to a corporation. When you lease assets to a corporation, the business pays a lease or rental fee, and you can claim the rental income. Doing this allows you as the lessor to deduct acquisition interest, depreciation, repairs and maintenance, insurance, and administrative costs.

> *[E]very man to whom God has given riches and wealth, He has also empowered him to eat from them and to receive his reward and rejoice in his labor; this is the gift of God. – Ecclesiastes 5:19*

When buying or building, purchasing a property in a historic or enterprise zone can be very monetarily beneficial. For example, there are tax and loan benefits because cities are always looking for ways to improve properties and create more opportunities to attract people. Once more people are attracted to a city or town, more properties are improved, and the city or town earns more tax money. Therefore, it is always important to do your research on different states and towns, particularly in terms of historical and enterprise zones; follow this direction and discover that you are an entrepreneur who can make a difference in the business world.

I live a clear and spiritual life and believe that God always has a plan for my direction. When my historical building lead me into the direction of commercial real-estate, that blew my mind. I kept that historical building for eight years and eventually leased my salon space to state attorneys. This led me into the direction of building a new, 9,500 ft^2 building for my salon and spa. 4,000 ft^2 are used for my spa, and 5,500 ft^2 are used for my salon. The rest of the building is leased to a beautiful café and coffee shop and to a fitness center.

Also, I finally decided to sell the historical property, which led me into other ventures. I had originally purchased the historical property for $168,000 and sold it for $510,000. This gave me a very nice gain, which provided me with the opportunity of buying more real-estate, so I purchased a twenty-unit apartment complex and a beautiful six-bedroom and five-and-a-half-bathroom beach house in the Outer Banks in North Carolina. By reinvesting in a 1031 tax-free exchange – which is a program through the government that allows investors to reinvest their profits within a certain timeframe, which is forty-five days to identify your property and 180 days to close the deal – this helped me in a capital gains savings.

My North Carolina House

The reason why I'm sharing this personal information with you is to demonstrate that if I – who came from a poor family consisting of my parents and four of us children all of whom were adopted from different families – can do this in the real-estate world, you can too. I don't believe in luck. I believe that the Lord provides us in the walk in his belief knowing that anything can be accomplished in his eyes.

> *I am the LORD your God; walk in My statutes and keep My ordinances and observe them. Sanctify My sabbaths; and they shall be a sign between Me and you, that you may know that I am the LORD your God. – Ezekiel 20:19-20*

Life – wow! It is everything. Life is our walk with our Father. Knowing that he is with us daily gives me the drive and motivation to make a difference in people's lives. You can make this difference too.

As demonstrated by my growth in the world of real-estate, we have the opportunity in life to give so much back to so many people. For example, my real-estate growth helped my staff of my salon and spa; I was in a position to offer better education and a very beautiful workplace. I want to help you grow in the business world too! I have more information to share, so please contact me for assistance with getting your business started!

A Stylist's Station in My Current Salon & Spa

An Area of My Spa in My Current Salon & Spa

Notes

Chapter 5: Build-Out Cost

A build-out cost is the cost you spend preparing a space for your business. It is necessary to plan for a build-out cost when designing your business. There are times that you can negotiate your build-out cost with your landlord, but this will increase your cost per square foot. This can also increase the terms of your rental space so that the landlord can get their return back on their investment.

Pretend you are about to set up your business in a new construction which has nothing but four, square walls. You have to do all the build-out. However, you could easily use 40% of your budget to complete part of the space before you start the build-out of your specific business space. Therefore, you need to remember to be careful and that rental space is negotiable. For example, you could negotiate with your landlord because you may want the rest of the shell of the property, meaning the drywall on the walls, to be completed at the landlord's cost instead of yours. Even if your landlord completes the drywall, you will still have to prime and paint the walls to start your business build-out.

> *Be careful because it is easy to go over budget! Keep in mind that you can always change accessories later when your budget is stronger.*

You can also negotiate the cost per square foot based on the improvements you make to the property. Remember that everything is negotiable. For example, when you build out your space, you can use less expensive fixtures, such as faucets and lights, and can use the money you save toward nicer floors, cabinetry, or other items that you think are more important to your business.

Cost is everything. When I started my first salon, my budget was $25,000, and I exceeded this budget by $10,000. I was shocked. I looked at my facility and wondered where all of the money had gone. The unexpected increase in costs was a result of upgraded tile floors and fixtures and me not being more careful with my budget. However, when I bought my historical building, I completed the renovation in four phases which allowed me to spread out the costs. More recently, when I built my current salon and spa, I went $100,000 over budget because the land it was built on was in poor condition! Like this piece of land, there are many property areas that are unpredictable. I did not expect to exceed my budget by that much, so my advice to you is to be careful and expect that there may be additional, *unexpected* costs.

When calculating your expected build-out costs, it is important to make a list. Write out the individual expenses you expect to incur and try not to miss anything in order to avoid unexpected costs later. It is one thing to dream, but, as one of my mentors said to me when I was preparing to build my first building, "My friend, your dream is too big. Dream about your building, but don't go too far outside of your budget range." He was right! I was way outside of my budget range, and, if I had not taken his advice, the result would have been devastating on my company. This personal experience not only relates to build-out costs, but it also serves as a reminder to listen to your mentors; they will help guide you to success.

It is so important to me that you reread the chapters in this book and remember that, as entrepreneurs, we are all in this world of business together; this is why I believe we should share as much information as we can to help each other become successful. I share my information with you to make sure that you have the opportunity to visualize your own direction in business and real-estate. I want you to realize how important it is to be cautious with the money you spend preparing a piece of property for your business. Finally, remember that when you invest in someone else's property, you are improving their property for the future.

My mission is to help you save in your costs when it comes to your business ventures. I am so excited to help each and every one of you save money, particularly when it comes to your build-out costs.

Notes

Chapter 6: Equipment Costs and Improvements

Before purchasing the necessary equipment and material for your business, list all of your expected costs in an organized fashion. This way, you will know how much each piece of equipment and material costs ahead of time. Calculating these costs may take some time, though. For example, you may have to contact different vendors and equipment supply companies to compare their prices. While this requires you to plan properly, it may save you as much as 10-30% on your purchases.

Remember that creating a plan for your company can save you so much when it comes to your budget, especially because it is so easy to go over budget. In today's market there are so many vendors and choices of products, and these many options provide ways for you to reduce your equipment costs.

It is so important to understand how to save money when it comes to purchasing equipment for your business. I was able to save money on the equipment costs for my salon and spa because I effectively used the resources available to me and shopped for my equipment. Specifically, I came from a family who didn't have much, so my dad and I built almost everything – cabinets, shampoo units, and the receptionist desk – in my first salon.

Fun Fact from Forbes' Reports: As of 2012, 61% of global internet users research products online. Additionally, 44% of online shoppers begin by using a search engine, and 75% of online shoppers never scroll past the first page of search results.

In terms of effectively shopping for equipment for my current salon and spa, I contacted cabinetmakers and asked for estimates for station retail centers, color cabinets, and shampoo cabinets. I compared costs in many ways. Specifically, for stylists' work stations, I contacted three companies and received bids from each for $1,200, $1,009, and $1,095 per station. However, I asked my cabinetmaker if he would be interested in building the stations and what he would charge. He offered a bid of $275 per station! I paid much less than I would have if I had accepted one of the first three companies' bids. Also, because the cabinetmaker does not specialize in stylists' stations and built them from scratch, I was able to choose from various textures and colors that would not have otherwise been options. I checked with more companies about other items I needed to purchase for my salon. For example, the cost per chair for styling chairs for an entire salon can be very high. One of the first companies I contacted about styling chairs priced them at over $695 per chair. I researched other options and bought styling chairs for $195 each!

Sinks, Chairs, & Cabinets for Hair Color in My Current Salon

Hair Drying Stations in My Current Salon & Spa

When purchasing equipment for a salon, there is more to consider than simply whether it is visually aesthetic. When choosing floors, for example, there are many designs and thousands of options, but don't forget that your stylists need to be comfortable while working. I considered this when purchasing floors. Not only did I test floors for comfort, but I researched whether particular floors would become stained if hair color were dripped or spilled. This is an important consideration with salon floors because, even though you might spend thousands of dollars on beautiful floors, one drop of color could stain them. I know this from personal experience; hair color was dripped on the floor of my salon in the historical building, so I refinished the flooring there every two years. Because of this experience, I purchased high quality laminate flooring for my current salon. This flooring is beautiful, and the padding underneath is triple-layered, which makes the floors comfortable for stylists and customers. My flooring is also stain-resistant and has a twenty-five year warranty.

Particular areas in salons can quickly lose their visual appeal, so these areas need extra consideration. For example, not only do salon floors need protection from potential stains, but the walls around hair color areas need to be protected. Any areas with 'heavy traffic,' such as entrance ways and waiting rooms, need special attention because they are used and viewed the most. Remember that guests look at *everything* when they are in salons whether they are sitting in waiting rooms or lying back while having their hair washed.

Spend your money wisely to make your salon visually appealing and take the time to look at your salon as if you are a customer there. Is it somewhere you would want to go? Walk through the entrance way. What do you immediately notice? If this were the first time you had ever entered your salon, would your impression be a positive one? Asking yourself these questions can help you figure out what areas of your salon need more attention.

Don't forget that you need to keep your salon and spa updated. To do this, you should touch up the paint in your business every two years. When you update your equipment, you can donate your older equipment to a local vocational school or a charity. When you donate equipment, such as chairs or shampoo bowls, you will usually receive a tax break.

If you remodel your salon, have another grand-opening of your new space. Invite your town or city's chamber of commerce, your customers and friends to your opening. Take advantage of this remodel as much as you can, but remember to always be honest with your business ventures.

In order to maximize your salon's growth, whether you are opening your salon for the first time or after a remodel, make sure to take a moment to sit down and look around. What does it need? More pictures? Updated brochures? Print materials? Invest in your company. Travel to salons and spas outside of your area. By looking at other salons, you will find ways to improve your own. Remember that improving your business does not mean simply updating the paint on the walls. You need to constantly think about what you can do to improve your business so that your customers believe in your company as much as you do.

If another salon in your area has a grand opening, your clients may find the new or updated salon more attractive than yours. Your staff may also see this other salon as an opportunity for better business, and you might run the risk of losing your staff members to this other facility. (Don't get me wrong, competition is good; it keeps us consciously aware of our surroundings.) As owners, our staff members want to believe in us. They want to know that we are strong leaders, who are willing to improve our business. They want to believe that we will invest in our facility as well as in them. As owners, we need to do this; we make sacrifices to build our employees' faith in us as leaders.

Business owners are especially busy, and personal lives and other commitments can sometimes get in the way of business commitments. I watched this happen with another business. My wife and I went to a well-known local restaurant for dinner. While we were looking forward to eating at the restaurant, we were disappointed. The food and service were amazing. However, the facility was not updated; it needed new paint, decorations, and, overall, more character. This was sad to us because, with some improvements to the facility, the restaurant could be even better and attract more customers. This is why it is important, even when life gets in the way of your business, to remember that you chose to own a company. Do not throw away everything that you have created because your walls need a coat of paint or your styling stations need good cleanings. You can even save money on these small improvements by being creative. For example, offer a part-time cleaning position to a current employee or a client who loves to clean in exchange for salon and spa services. In the business world, it is necessary to be creative to save money; I call this being innovative.

Take the time to improve your salon and spa, or watch your clientele disappear. Remember that there is always another salon that is newer and can offer more to your customers and employees. One rule I live by is to take the time to look around your business from the perspective of your clients. Additionally, never be afraid to invest in your future and in your team. It took many years for me to understand this, but, once I did, my salon exploded with business. Finally, as I have said and will keep saying, "Have a business plan!"

Notes

Chapter 7: Choosing Your Products

When purchasing products for your salon, check with various companies to see what they have to offer you as a customer. Keep in mind that you will be distributing their product lines, so you want to know why their products will benefit you.

Always look to the future for your business, even when choosing your products. Try to buy products from a distributor that will help your salon over time. Look for product companies that give back to the salons and spas to which they sell their products and sell products that are not diverted. Diversion of the products that you choose to sell can be detrimental to your business. Diverted products are sold at drug stores and other stores; this takes revenue away you're your employees as well as your business. Diverted products are not exclusive, are easily attainable, and their quality may not be guaranteed. I considered this advice when choosing a company from which to buy products. I decided to choose a company that gives back to my salon, while also making a profit from its retail.

For my salon I chose John Amico Educational Concepts, which is one of the largest family-owned hair care companies in the United States. It is the first multilevel company in the market. (In simple terms, "multilevel" means that the company sells its products to salons, like mine, who sell them to customers as well as to other stylists and salons; then, both the parent company, in my case John Amico Educational Concepts, my salon, and other salons that sell the products all make money from the sales.) This company gives a percentage back for all that I purchase from them. Because of this, in 2013 alone, I was able to give bonuses of over $5,000 to my team. Just imagine being able to give your team more incentives through monetary bonuses.

I have researched and contacted many product companies in order to find the best opportunities for my business, and I have been particularly pleased with this company. The company sent me a trial kit, which sat in my closet for about two years before I opened it. I needed to do something about the choices of color in my salon, so I decided to use the products from the kit. Needless to say, I was pleased with the products I tried.

John Amico is a great company because of its products and its mission to provide excellent products to its customers. Specifically, "John Amico is a recognized leader in the beauty industry, where protection and safeguard of the professional is our highest mission." The company "pledge[s] to provide the finest salon-exclusive products to make our members and their clientele happy. We develop successful business relationships through genuine care, mutual trust and respect – offering professionals an opportunity to achieve their fullest potential by helping other professionals. John Amico makes a difference in enriching professionals' lives."

> *The quality of your salon's products is very important.*

All of the John Amico hair color comes from Italy. You do *not* want to carry products sold in drugstores and large box stores. Carrying easy-to-purchase-anywhere products makes your salon less competitive. For my salon, I prefer Color Heads from John Amico's product line because it is an ammonia-free hair color from a line of products without harmful chemicals. Additionally, Jalyd Cream Color covers hair exceptionally well while making it shine for weeks. Also, for the developer, we use enzymes, which are made up of proteins – which protect the condition of hair and helps with longevity of hair color – and *not* peroxide, which is corrosive on hair fiber.

I feel that we, as salon owners, are doing our customers an injustice if we don't offer them something special. As professionals, we need to unite in our professional beliefs, and it is our responsibility as owners and leaders to help our teams and businesses grow by using the best products for our customers.

When you are the leader of a business, you need to take charge and be conscientious of the products and color-lines your business uses. Always research product distributors. Look at the product lines distributors sell, ask whether they are diverted lines, and determine whether these products would benefit your business more than others. As entrepreneurs, we constantly need to think of creative ways to keep our teams motivated, and money talks, which is why savings, such as those my company receives by using John Amico, can be so beneficial.

When choosing a product line, think about how many hair care companies there are in the beauty industry and why some are better than others. Review what each company has to offer, especially when it comes to education for your team. Considering this has been especially important to me and my company. I purchased products from a very well-known company for twenty years, and, when a large corporation bought them, my business' numbers changed. Specifically, the product retail sales in my salon dropped from 16% to 6% in six months! This is why, as owners, it is important to think about how we can increase retail sales, whether this is through switching product companies or creating incentives for our customers to buy products at our salons. Otherwise, clients may go to drug stores or large box stores to buy their hair products.

> *Taking the time to research products for your business can be extremely beneficial, especially when it comes to education that different companies offer.*

Try not to be overwhelmed by the many products and companies on the market. Always remember that, as entrepreneurs, we are very busy trying to be innovative. Take one step at a time, create a plan, and don't be afraid. You should be *excited* knowing that you have opportunities to make a difference. I want to make a positive difference for you and your company too, so please contact me with questions about how I can help you find wonderful products for your business. You and your company deserve only the best!

Notes

Chapter 8: Choosing Employees

Subject to the type of company you may be ready to open, you need employees – the right employees – in order to be successful. *Employees can make or break your business*, particularly if you are in the customer service industry. Even after you hire the right employees for your business, you need to have a company handbook and a mission statement explaining to your employees and your customers what is important to you about your business.

When I look for amazing stylists, I hold auditions. These auditions are used to assess individual talent. Prospective employees must successfully complete three interviews in order to be hired at my salon. The first interview is a traditional, oral interview at which time I want to learn about prospective employees' short and long-term career goals. The second part of my hiring process is a demonstration by a prospective employee that he or she can successfully complete a male haircut, a female haircut, a color service, an up-style, and finish work. This gives me and my stylists an opportunity to see a prospective employee's technical abilities. We also pay very close attention to a prospective employee's personality during this process.

Finally, a prospective employee must complete an interview with my entire team because he will be working with the team if he is hired. This interview is much more of a group interaction than a prospective employee being questioned by a panel. When a prospective employee interacts with my team, we learn a lot more about this person.

To find employees for your businesses, websites such as Indeed, Monster, and CareerBuilder, can link you with résumés and great hiring prospects.

Personality is a huge consideration when it comes to employees. I refuse to consider hiring someone if he or she has a bad attitude or a major ego; these are signs that a person lacks self-confidence, and, over time, this person can create extremely negative energy in your business. This is also true for *all* other positions of employees that we hire.

> *The old saying, "One bad apple can ruin the bunch," very much applies when it comes to hiring employees.*

I learned the hard way that you cannot change someone if he or she is not willing to change. You do not want to hire someone and hope that her attitude improves. Hiring someone with a bad attitude or ego can be disastrous to your company and might cause you to have to pay unemployment if you let her go. I have a golden rule in my company: I will give a new employee twenty-five to twenty-eight days to make me believe that she will be perfect for my team.

> *Always have a plan in place – like my three-step interview process – to hire amazing people. Life will throw you many curveballs, so keep your standards high, stick to your faith, and God will guide the right people to your company.*

Do not forget that you are in charge of your business, and it is your responsibility to coach and lead people to success. You can help change the lives of your employees if you are a caring and responsible leader; you can take a beautiful soul and change his or her life and walk. *Don't* limit yourself by immediately eliminating prospective employees. Offer auditions to many people and look at every aspect of these prospective employees and their talents.

My team and I offer free presentations on our industry at vocational and beauty schools. We allow students to come and shadow us to learn more about the industry. This helps make prospective employees feel more comfortable, especially if they have never worked in a salon or spa. Remember that new employees may feel intimidated and uncomfortable, so it is important for them to have coaches who will guide them and lead them in the right direction. New employees need training, and I treat every employee as if he or she is a student with very little knowledge who has the opportunity to learn and grow. When I see a new employee's progress, I start building more confidence in this person.

> *Every person you hire is a reflection on your company. Employees need to believe in your mission and meet your standards. Whether you own a small salon or a large facility, you need to set high standards for yourself and your employees.*

As leaders and entrepreneurs, we can help many people grow and provide them with opportunities to succeed. This is why it is necessary to have events to find new employees. For example, a career night can be beneficial because you can advertise your business and give prospective employees tours of your facility. Prospective employees get excited when they see that your business has a lot to offer them, and this gives them – and me – hope and inspiration.

Always be cautious and never become desperate when hiring your team. When hiring, you are not simply trying to fill a station or your salon. It is always better to set a high standard and follow it! I have friends who own salons and spas who have become desperate when hiring. However, *don't* hire someone just because she walks into your salon and says that she is a licensed stylist, manicurist, or massage therapist. Be cautious; complete background-checks on prospective employees and contact their references. Additionally, when conducting interviews, make sure to write a list of questions ahead of time and *don't* be afraid to ask too many questions.

Once I hire new stylists, I need to make sure to provide them with the necessary training to be successful. I usually have a small group of new stylists who need more training and experience. Once a week, I bring models into my salon for my new stylists. I spend quality time with each of them and assist them while they work with the models. Helping them with consultations is especially important. They need to have amazing verbal skills because communication is one of the keys to a successful business. If communication between a stylist and a customer fails, then cutting skills, coloring techniques, and finishing skills fail also. Additionally, there are so many different tools in salons, and stylists need to know how to properly use these tools. For example, I make sure that new stylists know how to use round brushes properly.

I love coaching and have a passion for helping others succeed. As entrepreneurs, we need to help others on our path and teach them how to succeed.

Sometimes owners feel like they lose control when it comes to their employees. However, as an owner, you should always be in charge. You took charge of your business when you opened it; your employees did not.

In the world of leadership, we have to view everything about people, numbers, and finding the correct people to also become amazing leaders; we have to find the right people for our businesses to become successful leaders. Great leaders need to look for other great leaders because you cannot do everything with your business by yourself. Leaders need other leaders!

Notes

75

Chapter 9: Marketing

Once you have built-out your space, installed the necessary equipment and product displays, and hired employees, you need to market your business. I always recommend having a marketing plan four weeks prior to opening your business. You need to have time to build up the excitement of your grand opening with the use of social media, local newspapers, and press releases with local television stations. You want to show customers what your business has to offer, especially if your business is service-oriented. You may want to have a grand opening when your business first opens, *or* you might want to wait a few weeks after opening in case there are any kinks (as I call them) to work out in your business.

> *Marketing is an ongoing process. You should never stop marketing your company. I always believe that you have to be in your company and work with your employees and customers in order to be successful and to market successfully.*

Social media can be vital to the growth of companies in my industry. In my business, my employees and I post three times per day on our business' Facebook page. We are able to book new clients for haircuts and colors by marketing to them through social media. By successfully using social media, my business is on the leading edge of marketing.

In today's market 84-90% of marketers use social media. As a business owner, social media is so easy to use because it allows you the opportunity to have thousands of viewers at your fingertips. Facebook, Twitter, Instagram, and Pinterest can all be used to successfully market businesses.

Facebook is an especially important marketing tool for today's businesses. As of 2012, 75% of marketers say that Facebook is critical or important to their businesses. Social media outlets other than Facebook can also be successful marketing tools. As of April 2012, Google reports that Google + now has 170,000,000 active users. Additionally, Pinterest is now the third most popular social network in the United States in terms of user traffic. Pinterest engages and retains users as much as two to three times more efficiently than Twitter did at a similar time in its business history. Daily Pinterest users have increased by more than 145% since the beginning of 2012. As of February 2012, Pinterest had accumulated 10,400,000 users.

Additionally, newly released studies show that 72% of internet users trust online reviews as much as personal recommendations. Also related to online reviews, 34% of consumers turn to social media to express their feelings about businesses. Online reviews of businesses uplift sales by an average of 18%. Additionally, shoppers are 105% more likely to purchase a product or service from a business after reading a positive review about it.

I was shocked when I first saw the statistics about how many reviewers look at social media as a way to rate a company. I can see why, though. Prospective clients want to choose salons, spas, or any other places of business that have true value; they want to go to businesses that make them want to spend their money. Additionally, these statistics demonstrate that marketing can have a great effect on your business. This is why it is so important to do your research. Search other businesses online and find ways to set your business apart from others. Keep in mind: what, where, and why. Why should the consumer choose your facility? What makes you different? Where do you stand out in the industry when it comes to reputation?

> *We have to set our business standards high so that we can be number one in consumers' eyes. Never give up and remember that our companies can always improve.*

Marketing is such a vital part of a successful company. My team and I brainstorm together in order to create new ways to better market the business. You do not need to a big team to be successful, though. If you are a small facility, surround yourself with amazing mentors. Set up conference call meetings quarterly. Don't think that you have to be a large conglomerate to create market strategies.

You can be a successful marketer regardless of the size of your business, and one way to do this is to really embrace the idea of using social media for your business. Salon and spa owners are always looking for new ways to grow clientele, and the best way to do this is to communicate with current and potential customers. At my salon and spa, my employees and I send out daily emails through a company called MailChimp, which provides customers with a list of openings and remaining services with the salon and spa staff. This gives clients receiving the email first-rights to book their appointments at a discounted price. They receive 10-20% of of their services, and this gives the salon and spa employees opportunities to sell-off all of their services. I always believe that embracing marketing opportunities, such as this one, can take companies to the next level.

> *When I first entered the industry in 1981, it was a different world. Clients would flood salons to receive services, so marketing was not as necessary. When I started my first company, I was twenty-one years old, and I had no experience with marketing. I want to share what I have learned about marketing with each and every one of you so that you can grow your businesses too.*

I have over thirty employees, and they all market the business differently. For example, one of my new talents posts every up-do and color she creates on Facebook. She gets amazing reviews every time and successfully markets herself as a stylist as well as the salon. Many of my staff members are very, successfully busy, but some who are still growing their clientele embrace social media and other marketing techniques.

Remember that the key to marketing, as well as many other aspects of a successful business, is to have a plan. For part of my marketing plan, my employees and I offer a rewards program, which gives our clients opportunities to earn credit for each dollar they spend on our services. They see value in our complimentary programs, such as this one, and it encourages them to return to the business. Creating incentive programs, such as those in which customers receive points or card punches, benefits your customers and your business. Additionally, at my salon and spa, we have a very successful referral program with major incentives for our guests. We provide our customers with opportunities to earn additional points by liking our Facebook page, tagging us on Twitter, and reviewing us on sites such as Google and Yelp.

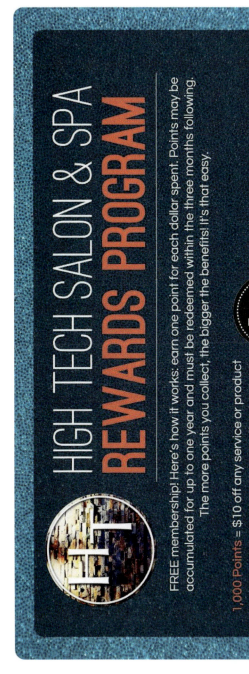

Your Name

Phone

Email

Stylist/Spa Specialist's Name

Friend's Name

Phone

Email

High Tech Salon & Spa
11 Green Hills Dr. Verona, VA 24482
540.248.3333   www.hightechsalon.com

Introduce us to new friends and we'll give them **a gift of $10 off** their first service at High Tech!

For every new guest who brings this card into the salon, we'll give YOU a **$10 credit**, too!

Jessie Wickersham is the graphic designer for High Tech Salon & Spa's Rewards Program and Referral Program.

With my salon and spa's marketing programs in place, my employees and I are blessed to see over eighty new clients every month. Not only are we gaining new clients, but we have a 92% client retention rate. Our points program and other incentive opportunities contribute greatly to this retention. We also sell an average of $125,000 of gift certificates per year, and this number tends to increase.

I am not bragging on my company's accomplishments. I just want you to see what you can do for your company to have the same business growth. It does not matter if you have one stylist or 1,000 staff members; you have the same opportunity as the salon and spa down the street, so pursue your business. I frequently say, "Don't wait for the business to come to you. You need to go after it to be successful." It is imperative for you to find new ways for your company to grow, and, as I have stated, to do this you need to make a plan. Open your eyes to every opportunity facing you today, and I promise that you will succeed in so many ways. Have amazing faith, be the best leader you can possibly be, and never give up.

Notes

87

Chapter 10: Financial Planning

Preparing a financial statement is necessary for your business. A financial statement puts your finances in order and provides your lenders with information about your finances and collateral. Before you borrow money from them, banks want to see your assets and your liabilities, and, in today's market, banks and other lenders are especially cautious when it comes to lending money. When providing a bank or other lender with your financial statement, not only will they want to know about your expenses, collateral, assets, and liabilities, but they will also want three years of tax returns and a copy of all of your investments. They especially want to see where you are getting your income.

When you are first introducing a loan from a private lender or a family member, you might not be sure how to handle the loan's interest rate or terms. This is why it is important to always do your research with existing lenders to find out what the going interest rates for loans are. This way you can offer a good interest rate to your investor(s).

Lenders will study your prospective business to determine if they think it can survive and be successful. Lenders just want to be paid back, and they want to know that you are financially secure enough to pay your debts. Lenders usually want you to pay 15-

20% down on a loan to show that you are invested in your business and that you are putting money in your business. Remember, banks are businesses too, and there is more than one of them in the market. You should search for the best terms and rates for your company.

When I first started my business venture, I visited three different lenders. Two of them said, "No," but one said, "Yes." When my first lender agreed to my loan, I had to have a cosigner on the note, but this was exactly what I needed; all I wanted was someone to give me a chance. As business owners, we strive to grow, and, when we choose to open companies, we want lenders to see what we can provide for the business market and to consumers and to give us a chance to do this.

Lenders look at new businesses as potential liabilities and not as assets. This is okay because, as entrepreneurs, we are driven. With the proper motivation, nothing can get in the way of success, so *don't* be fearful. Be aggressive and positive. Prove to yourself that you can succeed. This is what I did, and you can do it too. Remember, lenders have different applications and formats for financial statements. The one I provide below is applicable for all lenders.

There are also other lenders who help small businesses get started. Specifically, the Small Business Administration (SBA) can assist you with some of the financial aspects of starting your own business. The

SBA has very strict rules when it comes to lending money, but their goal is to help small businesses. For more information on the SBA, go to SBA.gov.

Notes

Chapter 11: Daily Operations

Regardless of the size of your company, you need to start your business the correct way (even if you have only one employee). You have invested in your business, and you want it to succeed and grow. If you use appointment books to organize your business' schedule, you will *not* have the information that is necessary for your business' growth. If your company is automated, reports generated based on the information you and your employees enter can be very valuable to you.

> *Success faces us every day, but it is what we want to do with it that matters.*

There are many software companies you can use to organize your business' information and schedules. Some of these include Salon Tec, Mikal, Millenium, Salon/Biz, and Envision. There are so many out there, but you need to research them to find out which one is the best for your company. Remember, you want your business to grow, but in order for this to happen, you need to plan properly for the future.

Like updating the fixtures, paint, and other equipment in your business, it is sometimes necessary to update your software. I learned the hard way that I had outgrown my method of organization and scheduling. I used an appointment book for my salon, and one day it just disappeared out of the salon. Whether you are using an appointment book or an automated system, *be careful* with your business information. Using an automated system generally allows you set passwords to protect your investment. I purposefully use the word "investment" because, when an employee works for your business, he or she is building a clientele from your reputation, not just from individual, hard work. It took me many years to understand this. I spent twenty-five years building my company's reputation before I became cautious of the fact that employees may join your company in order to build from your company.

You need to track everything in business. Watch your inventory very closely because you don't want inventory shrinkage. Inventory shrinkage occurs when employees take items home and do not pay for them. This can cost you thousands of dollars in losses. Other hidden costs in your salon can cause you to lose money as well. Sometimes too much product is used and is poured down the drain. Employees may not know how to mix products properly. Make sure that you coach them on how to use products correctly, or this may cost you thousands of dollars!

> *When you look at your company as a whole, try to envision all of your potential opportunities.*

If you have a level system, in which stylists are considered to be on different levels depending on their skills and professional experiences, watch each price point to make sure your employees are charging customers properly. Employees may want to lower their prices for particular customers, but they sometimes forget that they work for a company. In my salon, I have a level system for employees, and, if they set their price point goals with us during their reviews, then they cannot give their services away for free or for less than their set goals. This does not mean that we will not offer a form of discount that will help a particular person, though.

I explain to my employees that we cannot give everything away for free because, if we did, there would not be a business. Some of you may be thinking, "I would rather keep my business small in order to minimize headaches like these." However, you will have headaches and issues to work through in your business regardless of whether it is small or large. If you are a true entrepreneur, you will look at these headaches or challenges as *opportunities*.

Daily activities in my salon and spa include:
- Haircuts for males, females, and children
- Hair colors
- Styles
- Root retouches (and some foils)
- Manicures and pedicures
- Massages
- European facials
- Microdermabrasion
- Various body treatments

All of these services create revenue for my company. Additionally, it is very important to understand the value of retail. By selling retail items, such as shampoos, conditioners, hair sprays, and conditioning treatments, your business' profit margin can increase substantially.

You want your employees to succeed, and keeping their success in mind should be part of your daily activities as a business leader. I strongly believe that the growth of your employees' success has a major reflection on the growth of your company. I am a big believer that if you help people get what they need, it will help you get what you need.

> *"From the God of your Father who helps you, And by the Almighty who blesses you With blessings of heaven above, Blessings of the deep that lies beneath, Blessings of the breasts and of the womb" – Genesis 49:25*

In order for your daily activities to run smoothly, it is important to hire people who are coachable. You need to hire people who can take directions and use the information you give them to grow and succeed. (*See Chapter 8: Hiring for more information.*) I use the European level system in my salon in spa, which allows me the opportunity to pay different commissions for stylists' levels. Specifically, there are four levels in my salon: New Talents, Designers, Advanced Designers, and Master Designers. Employees' levels are determined by their experiences and individual evaluations. At each level, based on experience, my employees and I set a sliding scale to determine their commissions. Employees are evaluated by a number of factors, including verbal skills, marketing skills, cutting, coloring, finishing skills, massaging experience, years as an esthetician, experience as a manicurist and pedicurist, percentage of pre-booked appointments, percentage of retail growth and sales, and retention rate.

Not only do you need to keep track of your employees' skill levels, but you need to organize information about your clients and individual services and purchases. Specifically, the reports in my salon include information about the number of females and males who visit the salon and spa, customers' average number of visits per year, how much the average client spends, the number of new customers each year, retention rates of customers, prices and sales of services, number of services offered and sold, price and sales of retail items, and the number of retail items offered and sold. A collection of this information shows me that each part of my salon and spa is active in various areas of service and retail. Most importantly, this information shows up-sales. I have a standard in my company that, on a daily basis, I want to sell at least 90-95% of the services in the salon. My employees and I are successfully able to do this by sending daily emails to a customer list. Also, we have an Availability Board, which is an updated whiteboard in the waiting area of the salon, so all of our guests can see the salon's daily openings. Customers have an incentive to use these services on the whiteboard because they receive 10% off at the moment of service.

Remember, it is so important to track every area of your business on a daily basis!

I feel that it is God's plan for us to succeed as long as we choose to use our gifts from him wisely.

"Every good thing given and every perfect gift is from above, coming down from the Father of lights, with whom there is no variation or shifting shadow. In the exercise of His will He brought us forth by the word of truth, so that we would be a kind of first fruits among His creatures" – James 1:17-18.

Notes

Chapter 12: Building Success for Guest Coordinators

Guest or front desk coordinators can make or break your business. This is why it is so important to make sure that guest coordinators have proper training. Personality is incredibly important too.

A guest coordinator needs to have a great personality and be responsible. Think about when you and a friend go to a restaurant and eat amazing food. Even though the food is great, bad service can ruin your meal. This will make you question whether you should take another chance on going to the restaurant and spending your money there.

Guest coordinators *must* have marketing skills. They have opportunities to sell services and products that stylists and other employees do not because of their constant interactions with customers. When a guest coordinator is well coached in the marketing aspect of business, she opens herself up for so many opportunities and can help the company she works for grow so much.

Guest coordinators need to know proper phone etiquette, infer what guests' needs are, and offer guests professional experiences. As a guest, you have to agree that you want an experience that makes you feel like spending your money at a business is worthwhile.

Additionally, guest coordinators need to be focused. It should be expected that guest coordinators will be on task at work. I always say, "Dot every I and cross every T." Always cover all bases. Be willing and able to handle all situations. As a business owner, I love for someone to take charge in his or her specific business position.

A guest coordinator needs to be someone who is coachable; this is vital. At my company, I have weekly meetings with my guest coordinators to review what is working and what is not working. When I meet with them, I always embrace their ideas and opportunities for growth in our team. During meetings, we write ideas on my conference board, combine our talents and knowledge, and find ways in which the company can improve.

When my guest coordinators and I meet, I ask about their daily activities at the front desk. These activities center on taking care of our guests. For example, they offer guests cucumber and lemon water, which we make fresh daily, in glasses with crushed ice. Remember, it's the simple things like this that make a difference in guests' experiences at your business. Consumers pay attention to details and value these details; this can make you a fortune!

> *Focus on keeping your guests happy, and commit to your business so that it can be successful. This is your task as a leader!*

I value my staff and encourage you to value the employees in your companies too. When you run a company, you don't need to do your job alone: you have a team. Even if you are just one stylist in a salon, you can brainstorm with mentors or listen to educational CDs in your car. For example, I have multiple educational CDs in my car because I know that driving is a time for me to listen and learn. You can never learn enough!

> *If you need additional training help, there are training DVDs that can assist in your ventures with your guest coordinators.*

As a leader, you cannot be afraid to put issues on the table and have frequent discussions with employees. I am the leader of my team, but my team members have amazing ideas too. Many brains are better than one!

As a business owner for the last twenty-five years, I have learned to never stop raising the bar. I always say, "When we have picked all of the fruit from the lower branches, reach higher."

Notes

Chapter 13: Challenges & Statistics to Keep in Mind

Never forget your objective for choosing to open your company. This can be difficult, but, *don't* forget your mission! You can make a difference in the business world and in the lives of many people, so smile, get up, and say to yourself, "I can do this. I am making a difference in so many people's lives." We all need to do this at times. I know that I have said what you have probably thought from time to time: "Why did I take on this task?" Just remember that, as entrepreneurs, *we can make a difference*!

Some Major Findings from Forbes' Reports:

o *More adults are involved in business startups*. The percentage of adults involved in startups in 2012 hit 13%, which is a record high since Babson began tracking entrepreneurship rates in 1999.

o *Startups are viewed more as opportunities than necessities*. A majority of adults who started businesses in the past two years opened their businesses to pursue various opportunities rather than out of necessity.

o *People recognize that business opportunities exist.* Between 2008 and 2012, 56% of adults said they had the ability to start businesses, and, more recently, 43% of Americans believe that there are good opportunities for entrepreneurship. This number has increased by more than 20% since 2011, and it is the highest level recorded in the history of the study (which is called the Global Entrepreneurship Monitor U.S. Report).

o *Home-based businesses are hot.* 69% of new businesses in the U.S. started at home, and 59% of established businesses are home based.

o *People of all generations are taking chances on their own businesses.* About 15-20% of the workforce, regardless of age, is engaged in running a start-up or a more established business once labor-force participation rates for each generation are taken into consideration.

o *Immigrants are a major force on the entrepreneurial scene.* More than 16% of first-generation immigrants started or ran start-ups in 2012. This number is higher than the 13% participation rate for Americans who aren't immigrants.

○ *Women are still diving into entrepreneurship but have fallen behind men a bit*. For every ten men involved in entrepreneurship, there are seven women involved in entrepreneurship. This number has decreased since 2011 at which time there were eight women for every ten men involved in entrepreneurship. One factor contributing to this is that men's rate of new business creation increased while women's held steady.

○ *We've yet to tap the potential of global markets*. While the digital revolution has made it possible to reach customers overseas, only 12% of U.S. entrepreneurs have more than 25% of their clientele based abroad.

Review your company one step at a time. We all have challenges every day; this is why it's called "business," so take charge, don't show fear, be strong, and make it happen!

Notes

Chapter 14: Growing Your Profit Margin

There are so many ways to grow your company's profit margin. Dealing with overhead – meaning everything you have to pay for, such as electricity, supplies, employee pay, etc. – is always a challenge in the business world. Being able to reposition numbers is not difficult; it just takes time.

Some examples of how you can help with your overhead costs and building profits:
- Rent
- Payroll
- Supplies and products used in salon
- Utilities (including water and electricity)
- Salon and spa cleaning

Rent. This is an area subject to location. Rent can be reduced if you have been at a particular location for a while. Set up a time to meet with your landlord to discuss lowering your rent because it never hurts to ask if he or she would consider doing so. Before asking, though, make sure your landlord knows what improvements you have made to the property. Even if your rent is reduced by $200 per month, this saves you $2,400 per year.

Payroll. You have to be especially careful when it comes to this cost; it is needed, but you have to watch every angle of your money. I try to run my administration cost around 4-6% of the weekly payroll. Many companies can increase their administration costs when it comes to the number of their employees and how many assistants and administrative staff members work for the companies. In my salon and spa, I have five guest coordinators and four assistants, so, based on my income producers, each of us has a different mathematical plan. Study your company's numbers and create a plan that fits your company.

Supplies. This is an area that is so easy to adjust, particularly when it comes to your company's size and budget. I keep a close eye on my salon and spa's inventory, and doing this can save you a large amount of money and can add a lot to your bottom-line cost. Watch your turnovers on all of your product lines and watch how your staff members are promoting your business' products. There are times that you need to rotate retail lines too because clients are always searching for something new.

Utilities. In my company, I have invested in an on-demand gas and hot water system. I ran a cost expense on this unit, and, with the money it is saving my business, it will pay for itself in six months. This is an example of why you have to look at every angle of your costs. Also, recycle everything you can. We need to protect our companies and our country.

Products. I prefer for my employees to share their products because this reduces costs. The money saved from this can help with other expenses in the salon and spa. Keep your products organized and make sure that your business' products, whether these are hair color or retail products, are inventoried. For example, I had a color line in my salon, and the inventory was $19,000. I brought John Amico color into my salon, and this cost became $2,400. This price difference saved my business so much money. Also, because my company is using John Amico products, we receive a return, which helps to give the staff bonuses. To date, our color line is around $7,500.

Salon and Spa Cleaning. Review different cleaning companies, but be very careful. If you try to save a lot of money in this area, you might lose clients. If clients see that your facility is not clean and that you are not investing in your facility, then they will spend their money elsewhere.

> *As entrepreneurs, we have to look at every area of savings possible in our businesses.*

<u>Notes</u>

Planning for Book #2

My second book will be all about marketing strategies and additional ways to grow your companies. I will also give you the opportunity to contact me so that I can help you develop a program for your company and increase your bottom-line. I have so much advice to offer young hairdressers about how to book and retain clients and change their ways of thinking about the hair industry. I will offer you the same advice and suggestions that I offer my staff!

Remember, in our industry, if you are not growing, you are dying.

Acknowledgments

- To my readers, thank you so much for taking the time to read this roadmap to business. God bless you all!
- Suzanne, my lovely wife, who has encouraged and inspired me to write this book and to help to make a difference in a lot of businesses
- Gracen, Spencer, and Victoria, my children – Remember that life is full of opportunities and to never let anyone steal your dreams
- My salon and spa team for teaching me so much in my years of business that has lead me to writing this book
- My parents, Agnes G. Back and James R. Back, for encouraging me to never be discouraged and to always give life my all and never stop growing
- John Amico Company for being an inspiration to the beauty industry
- Gordon Barlow for taking the time to believe in someone of young age, seeing his potential, and teaching him all about commercial real-estate
- Joanie Eiland – I was gifted the opportunity to have been taught and educated by a wonderful business woman who inspires me as an investor

and educator – thank you for being a great mentor and an amazing friend!

- o Russ Rutan for teaching me as a young man about commercial real-estate
- o Editor, Holly M. Rasheed for taking the time to position all of the wording in my book, I cannot thank you enough for this
- o Cover Designer, Aaron Tinsley for sharing your talents and creating a visual picture for the cover of my book
- o Cover Inspiration, Bryan Demory for giving me an initial vision and ideas for my front cover – You are an amazing artist!
- o Jessie Wickersham for spending quality time to email all of the data and pictures and for being an inspiring person in your creativity
- o Sir Richard Branson for inspiring me with his words and business ventures
- o Robert Kiyosaki for his inspiring quotes
- o Donald Trump for his inspiring words
- o Joel Osteen for always inspiring me with his enthusiastic biblical teachings
- o Tony Robbins for being an incredibly inspirational, motivational speaker and believing in people's potential

References

- The majority of the statistics in this book come from Forbes' Reports unless otherwise cited.
- I also use The Green Book for salon-and-spa-related statistics.

Relevant Websites:
- franchiseopportunities.com
- businessplanupdate.com
- legalzoom.com
- dictionary.law.com
- indeed.com
- monster.com
- careerbuilder.com
- sba.gov

My Contact Information:
tbackinvestor@gmail.com *or*
hightechsalon@gmail.com
Salon Number: (540) 248-3333
Salon Website: hightechsalon.com

Terry Back